IF MY CAT WERE A LION

IF MY CAT WERE A LION

by Yvonne Giba Svitlik

Xulon Press

Xulon Press
2301 Lucien Way #415
Maitland, FL 32751
407.339.4217
www.xulonpress.com

Paperback ISBN-13: 978-1-66285-423-1
Ebook ISBN-13: 978-1-66285-424-8

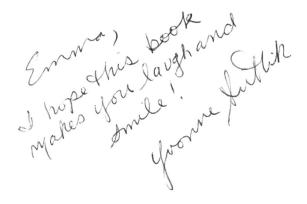

To my family, cat, and Sarah...

Thank you to my children and husband, Charles, for encouraging

me to adopt our little Honey the Cat.

I would like to especially thank my beautiful daughter Sarah.

She helped turn my idea into reality -

she helped me get this story into your hands!

If my cat were a lion,
it would let out a ferocious **roar,**

instead of a little,
tiny **meow-r.**

If my cat were a lion,
it would **nap way up in a tree,**

instead of **resting** cozily next to me.

If my cat were a lion,
it would **hunt its prey**,

instead of begging for food
ten times a day.

instead, its purr tickles my belly like **a tiny little mouse.**

If my cat were a lion,
it would **run through the plains,**

instead of **lazily looking through the window at the rain.**

If my cat were a lion,
it would be **protecting the cubs,**

instead of stealthily
sneaking into my tub.

If my cat were a lion,
it would be **climbing great rocks,**

instead of **running off with my socks.**

If my cat were **a lion** and it **kissed my face,**

I would get **knocked down right in that very place.**

If my cat were **a lion,**
I would be **squished by a cuddle,**
and most certainly **struggle.**

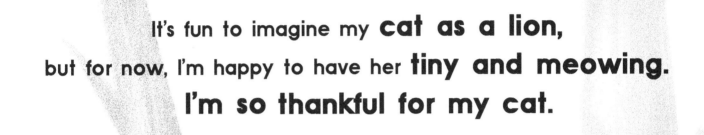

It's fun to imagine my **cat as a lion,**
but for now, I'm happy to have her **tiny and meowing.**
I'm so thankful for my cat.

CPSIA information can be obtained
at www.ICGtesting.com
Printed in the USA
JSHW042219050423
39965JS00006B/117

9 781662 854231

Illustrated by Firerr